Is That You, God?

Cindy Jacobs

Published by Generals International
P.O. Box 340, Red Oak, TX 75154
ISBN: 978-0-9861634-1-8

Library of Congress Cataloging-in-Publication Data
Jacobs, Cindy
Is That You, God? : Recognizing his voice above the noise / Cindy Jacobs p. cm.
22 21 20 19 18 17 16 15 2 3 4 5 6 7 8 9 10 11 12 1

Contents

Chapter One
God Wants to Speak to Me?

Do you ever feel like no matter what you do, God's voice seems silent? I know I have felt that way sometimes—beginning when I was a little girl.

Growing up in San Antonio, Texas, I didn't hear a lot about God's voice. I grew up in a proper, God-fearing, Southern Baptist home. My Daddy was a preacher, and he and my mother taught my brother, sister and me about Jesus' love and salvation. At our small Baptist church, we heard a lot about God's love, God's mercy, God's grace, and God's judgment—but not a whole lot about His voice directly.

You have to understand that I was an unusual child. I was four years old the first time I heard God's voice. Not too many mothers have to deal with their young child proclaiming that she was going to have a little sister—and being correct. And not only that, but to my parents' surprise, my little sister, Lucy, made her arrival within a few months of my bold proclamation! Of course, I used this accurate pronouncement to my best advantage, and as teenagers, I used it to make my sister beholden to me! (God had a bit of work to do in me in my teen years.)

But as a young lady in Texas during the 60s and early 70s, people didn't talk a lot about prophecy or hearing God's voice. For a long time, I felt like an outsider—alone in my experiences with the Lord when, at times, His small still voice would reveal things to me that I had no earthly way of knowing.

Why could I hear so clearly? For one, although my parents were not of an understanding that God spoke prophetically today, they did teach me to pray and to expect that God answered prayer. Being raised in that atmosphere, I took my parents at their word and grew in my faith as the prophetic gift began to bubble up inside me. Today, of course, there are wonderful churches, ministries, and movements that embrace biblical prophecy. As well, there are many excellent resources—including books, online teachings, sermons, and video materials—that help Christians develop their prophetic gifting.

Why This Book?

Do we need another book on hearing God's voice? Well, for one, I think that some material on prophecy is a bit mystical and hard to understand, or presumes a certain level of biblical knowledge on the part of the reader or listener. My purpose in putting together this simple, short message is to demystify the voice of God and, in a clear, understandable way, share how you can hear His voice more effectively and powerfully.

Now, you may be saying, "Sure, Cindy, that's easy for you to say. You are a prophet who travels around the world—you hear easily from God. Me? Not so much." You know what? I don't always hear clearly from God either! Also, there have been some dark times in my life when I wondered whether God was still speaking to me at all.

I want you to join with me to explore how we can better hear God's voice—together. Not only when you are sitting in church on Sunday morning, the cares of the world waiting just outside the doors of the church. I'm talking about the need to hear Him on Monday morning, when real life runs a red light and T-bones your spiritual life, sending you spinning in circles. For me, I really need to hear His voice the most when the spinning stops, and I'm battered and bruised. How about you?

Many of the things I will be sharing here you might have heard before. But sometimes, it's good to get a refresher (again, that goes for me, too!). Perhaps you are a new Christian or simply eager to learn about how God speaks today. If so, this might be the first time you have heard this news: God loves you, has a wonderful plan for your life, and wants to speak to you.

As I mentioned, the first time I heard God's voice, I was four years old. Since then, He has taken me on a "two steps forward, one step back" journey to attune my ear to hear His voice more clearly. And through all the proceeding years of walking with God and learning to hear Him more accurately, I have learned that He yearns to speak to all Christians. Why? Because He is our Father and loves us more than we can ever know.

God Desires Intimacy

Consider John 18, which tells of Jesus' last night before He was crucified. He stands—or kneels, hands bound—before Pontius Pilate, the representative of worldly power, backed by the might of Rome. As Pilate questions Jesus about whether or not He is the (earthly) king of the Jews, Jesus responds and says, "You say rightly that I am a king. For this cause I was born, and for this cause I have come into the world, that I should bear witness to the truth. Everyone who is of the truth hears My voice" (John 18:37).

Did you see what it says? Everyone who is of the truth (born again) hears His voice! That's you. That's me. And that is love! If you are a parent, you know what a delight it is to have a good talk with your child. You love them, adore them, and want to get to know them better, so you can help them and guide them. Think how much more, then, God wants the same with you.

The Lord wants to enter into deeper intimacy with you as you follow His way of love. I Corinthians 14:1 says, "Follow the way of love and eagerly desire gifts of the Spirit, especially prophecy" (NIV). What does it mean to follow the way of love, particularly in regard to hearing God's voice and the prophetic life?

Following the way of love simply means to do all things in love—especially when you tune in to hear God's voice. If that voice is harsh, condemning, or guilt-inducing, test the voice. Is it truly God's voice, or is it the world, the flesh, or the devil? Sometimes it's hard to tell, but in Chapter 2, we will go into greater detail about how to hear God's voice above all the other voices that assault your senses every day.

Now, there are definite biblical steps you can take to sharpen your ear to hear God more clearly, and we will get into those steps later in the book. But God wants to speak to you—if you are ready to listen. This is not a secret puzzle that God doesn't want you to solve;

He yearns to speak to you and to bring words of encouragement, peace, and yes, sometimes correction, into your life and heart.

All Are Called to Prophesy

Before we move on, it's important to state up front that while not every Christian is seated in the office of the prophet, every believer can prophesy. 1 Corinthians 14:39 says, "Therefore, brethren, desire earnestly to prophesy, and do not forbid to speak with tongues." Did you notice that Paul uses the word "brethren"? This word "brethren" refers to the entire church—it is God's will that all members of the church prophesy. There are some Christians who are specifically called to be prophets (and you may be one of those people), but all of us are called to hear His voice and share His loving message with those around us. Yes, that means He wants you to hear His voice and act upon it—today.

In the next chapter, we will explore how we can recognize God's voice above the buzz of all the other voices that surround us each day. The Bible will be our guide, and thankfully, it has much to say about when a "voice" is God's and when it might not be.

Chapter Two

How to Recognize God's Voice

"Why Can't I Hear God's Voice?"

This is one of the most frequently asked questions I receive from people I meet. And I hear it all around the globe, in the poorest nations to the wealthiest cities of Asia and Europe. All Christians—rich and poor, young and old—have the same desire and yearning to hear God's voice more clearly and frequently.

People approach me and say, "Cindy, I want to hear the voice of God." Or they say "I can't hear God's voice! Doesn't He love me?" You may be one of those people who have asked that second question (as well as the first). That's a great question, and thankfully, there is a solid answer: yes, God does love you!

Why do some people think they don't hear His voice? It's amazing to me how many longtime Christians I meet who don't know they can hear the voice of God. It's not that they struggle to hear His voice—they have never even been taught that they can! Therefore, they don't try. It's sad to me that some people don't know that God wants to reveal Himself to them. But He does! He wants to show us who He is, and there are certain ways that we can learn what God wants us to hear.

"How Do I Hear from God?"

Another question I'm frequently asked is, "If I'm going to hear the voice of God, how do I do it?" I mean, do you just get up in the morning and have a conversation with God? Well . . . yes, of course we can say that, in a way, hearing from God is a conversation. But it's about us listening for and to Him, and not just talking at Him. Some people would prefer it if God would just come up to them, tap them on the shoulder, and say, "Do not do that! You are going to be in big trouble if you do that."

I've had that "shoulder-tap wish" myself. When I was in high school, I would approach my Dad, who was a preacher, and say, "Daddy, I have to make a decision. But I don't want you to give me every theological reason in the Bible why I should do this. I have five minutes, so I need you to say 'yes, you can go' or 'no, you can't go.'" And my Dad would just smile at me and shake his head. Sometimes it worked, and he would give me a straight response. Life is complicated, however, and my Daddy was smart enough not to give me an unrealistic or simple answer to what were sometimes complicated issues in my life.

Sometimes we feel that way with God, don't we? We feel frustrated and impatient, and just want Him to say, "No! Don't marry that person! Big mistake!" Or, "Yes, take that job. That is my will." One of the reasons why God doesn't always answer in our timing and tone is that He wants us to grow spiritually. That's right! God wants us to grow up; therefore, He doesn't always make it easy because He wants us to learn to know His whispers—to become familiar with the timbre and tone of His voice.

It's human nature to communicate with the ones we love. For instance, when my grandchildren were in the womb, I indoctrinated every one of them to hear "grandma's voice." I understood that they had little ears at a certain stage in the womb and that they could hear me, so I would go speak to them in the womb. (My daughter and daughter-in-law can tell you some funny stories!)

It became really fun once we knew if it was a boy or girl, and I could start using their names. I'd say, "Hello, Malachi (my oldest grandchild), this is your favorite grandmother. You have other grandmothers, but I am your favorite." Do you think I need to repent of that? I don't know if that's considered taking too much "grandmother license," but I tell you what, those grandchildren love me! They came out of the womb knowing my voice.

You Are Wired to Hear God's Voice

And that is exactly what God wants to do with you: He wants you to hear the voice of the One who loves you immeasurably. He wants you to hear His voice clearly and without filters or static. In fact, we can read about His desire in the Bible. John 10:2-4 says:

> But he who enters by the door is the shepherd of the sheep. To him the doorkeeper opens, and the sheep hear his voice; and he calls his own sheep by name and leads them out. And when he brings out his own sheep, he goes before them; and the sheep follow him, for they know his voice.

First of all, biblically, we can stand upon the Word of God. One of the beautiful things about Pentecost was that all those who were filled with the Holy Spirit that day could hear His voice. Only the prophets could do so in the Old Testament, but God wants all of His children to be able to recognize when He speaks to us. In essence, you are already wired to hear His voice.

Before Jesus ascended to heaven, He comforted His followers by saying, "You have heard from Me; for John truly baptized with water, but you shall be baptized with the Holy Spirit not many days from now" (Acts 1:4-5). He continued on, saying, "You shall receive power when the Holy Spirit has come upon you; and you shall be witnesses to Me in Jerusalem, and in all Judea and Samaria, and to the end of the earth" (Acts 1:8).

A few days later, after Jesus had ascended to the right hand of the Father, His apostles and closest followers were gathered in the upper room to celebrate the Jewish Feast of Weeks, known in Greek as Pentēkostē (or Pentecost). While gathered there,

> They were all with one accord in one place. And suddenly there came a sound from heaven, as of a rushing mighty wind, and it filled the whole house where they were sitting. Then there appeared to them divided tongues, as of fire, and one sat upon each of them. And they were all filled with the Holy Spirit and began to speak with other tongues, as the Spirit gave them utterance.
>
> ACTS 2:1-4

As Jesus had promised, the Father had sent the Helper, the Holy

Spirit, to empower His church. In Peter's explanation of the startling and wondrous events of Pentecost, he said, "This Jesus God has raised up, of which we are all witnesses. Therefore being exalted to the right hand of God, and having received from the Father the promise of the Holy Spirit, He poured out this which you now see and hear" (Acts 2:32-33).

In his sermon to the people, Peter quotes from a prophecy given by the Old Testament prophet, Joel:

> And it shall come to pass in the last days, says God, That I will pour out of My Spirit on all flesh; Your sons and your daughters shall prophesy, Your young men shall see visions, Your old men shall dream dreams.
>
> ACTS 2:17

Pentecost was the first time that all Jesus' followers had received the Holy Spirit. Notice it does not say "some flesh" or "nearly all flesh," but all flesh. From the time of Pentecost, God released His Spirit to the church, to be our guide, protector, and helper.

And because of Pentecost, and God's gift of the Holy Spirit, all Christians now have access to hear the Father's voice. Even if you think you don't know His voice, when you accept Jesus Christ as your Lord and Savior—and especially when the power of the Holy Spirit manifests through you—you become Spirit-empowered. So, you know what? You are already wired to hear His voice.

The good news, then, is that the Spirit of God Himself is in you and me, so there is a conversation daily that can take place—if we pursue it and attend to it.

Now that you know that God can speak to you and wants to speak to you, here are the five basic ways He might speak to you. I am only going to touch on these five things briefly here, as we will be unpacking each one in greater depth throughout the book:

Scripture - As you study His Word, you will better be able to hear and discern His voice from all others.

Prayer - We need to both talk to and listen to God. It is not a one-way street; we must get to a quiet place without distractions, so we can better position ourselves to hear His still small voice. You may want to keep a prayer journal, capturing the impressions or words that you hear from God.

Another Person - God will sometimes speak through another person in order to exhort, edify, or comfort you. This is called personal prophecy, and we will address this aspect of hearing from God in chapter 6.

Circumstances - God uses the circumstances in our lives to speak to us. For instance, let's say you desire to tithe 10% of your income, but currently, your budget is short of that goal by $121. You pray; the next day, a friend calls to say they have a room for rent, and you realize that you will save $121 by moving. That's one example of God speaking to you through your circumstances.

Dreams and Visions - Though I won't go into details here, dreams and visions are also biblical ways that God can speak today.

Hundreds of books have been written on the ways in which God can speak to us. And while I wanted to mention them, I don't want to dwell here. My main goal in this book, rather, is to answer the question posed in the title itself: "Is that You, God?" To that end, let's now explore the critical issue of how to discern God's voice from other voices.

Discerning God's Voice

How can you know the difference between the voices from the world (and when I say "world," I am also including the voice of the enemy), your own internal voice, and God's voice? Sometimes it can be very difficult to discern between the three, and of course, hearing God more clearly is part of the life-long sanctification process. To "sanctify" means to be set apart for a purpose, and our purpose as believers is to grow in our walk with Christ so that He can use us more powerfully to reach others for Him.

First Thessalonians 5:23 says, "Now may the God of peace Himself sanctify you completely; and may your whole spirit, soul, and body be preserved blameless at the coming of our Lord Jesus Christ." God's desire is for our entire life (spirit, soul, and body) to glorify Him as we grow in intimacy with Him. A major part of our growth is found in recognizing and heeding the voice of our Shepherd (see John 10:4).

Even if you don't yet realize it, wired inside of you is the ability to hear the voice of God. In this section, I'm going to give you some specific points on how to test what you hear and how to know whether or not it is from God.

Is it Scriptural?

The Bible is the greatest tool we have to consistently and clearly hear from God. And here's some great news: The Lord will never violate what is written in Scripture. At certain times in life, most of us have been in a situation where we know a particular action or thought is contrary to Scripture, but we try still to rationalize the action. We might say, "Yes, but this situation gives me no other choice!" But it's important to know—there are no "right" situations like that. The Lord will never violate what is written in Scripture, and He will never approve of you doing so either.

God is never going to violate His own Word; the Bible is the manufacturer's handbook for all of creation. It is, literally, our manual for how we should live our life; therefore, it is primary.

In order to grow in your ability to hear God's voice, you need to become a student of His Word. By studying the scriptures—alone and with other Christians—you will get to know His nature and character. You can always tell somebody who is a diligent student of the Bible by the way they hear from God and how they share what He is saying to them. There will be a lot of scripture in what they say; the word of God will just pour out of them.

Also, does the prophecy display the character of Christ? Would God say that? Would God say to do that?

Not every voice we hear is the voice of the Holy Spirit. Consider this paramount scripture on the subject from 1 John 4:1-3:

> Beloved, do not believe every spirit, but test the spirits, whether they are of God; because many false prophets have gone out into the world. By this you know the Spirit of God: Every spirit that confesses that Jesus Christ has

come in the flesh is of God, and every spirit that does not confess that Jesus Christ has come in the flesh is not of God. And this is the spirit of the Antichrist, which you have heard was coming, and is now already in the world.

In other words, there are demonic voices that might attempt to whisper to you, and you need to be alert to that. Again, whether you are hearing the voice of the world, your own flesh, or the devil, you need to tune to the right channel because Satan doesn't even mind telling you he's God.

Did you know that? The devil doesn't mind using the name of God if he can deceive you. In my book *Deliver Us From Evil*, I talk about a Christian woman named Johanna Michaelsen who wrote *The Beautiful Side of Evil*. In this book, she talks about how she used to be into the New Age movement and had a spirit guide named "Jesus." And "Jesus" would come to her and tell her all sorts of things—but this wasn't the real Jesus, so the voice could not be trusted.[1]

When you are in prayer and you believe you are hearing from God, ask the Holy Spirit to confirm it by giving you an inner witness (I'll touch more on this below). Ask yourself, does the word fit the character of God, and is it in line with the scriptures?

Seek Fellowship

Surround yourself with people who do hear the voice of God. And if you don't have such connections, then ask God to bring them into your life. If you ask, God will do it. I remember when my little sister moved to Minnesota from Texas, and she would call me and say, "I don't have any friends." We made it a matter of prayer, and soon she was surrounded by many friends. God will give you people whom you can trust. The key is to be watchful and to embrace those new relationships when God brings them your way.

An Inner Witness: Resonance

Are you familiar with the physical principle of resonance? Objects have certain characteristic frequencies at which they vibrate. For example, if you cause a bell to vibrate near another bell with the same characteristic frequency and size, the second bell will vibrate and shake. In other words, the other object will begin to vibrate of its own accord. Likewise, when we hear the voice of God—either through a scripture that speaks to us, the word of a friend, or the "still small voice" of His presence—we experience resonance.[2]

Jesus Himself speaks of such resonance in John 10:27-29:

> My sheep hear My voice, and I know them, and they follow Me. And I give them eternal life, and they shall never perish; neither shall anyone snatch them out of My hand. My Father, who has given them to Me, is greater than all; and no one is able to snatch them out of My Father's hand.

In this passage, Jesus is making a distinction between the believers who hear His voice (who resonate with Him) and those who do not follow Him, whom He refers to elsewhere in John 10 as strangers, wolves, thieves, and robbers.

Notice that this passage—as well as much of John 10, where Jesus speaks about God as the Good Shepherd—says that the sheep hear His voice. For us today, it means that even though Jesus is not with us in bodily form, we can hear His voice and know for certain that it is indeed Christ. That is resonance.

Godly Counsel

It's not only important to surround yourself with mature believers who can guide you and correct you in how you hear God—godly counsel, but to also surround yourself with people who can be your "sounding boards." These can be peers, friends, a pastor, spouse, or another believer in whom you trust. Like those with whom you resonate, sounding boards are those closest to you who help you stay on a straight path when it comes to hearing from God. Of course, all of us have moments when we're tired and when we're weary. That is why we need godly accountability.

Years ago, my children attended a certain Christian school, and many in the school did not believe that women could be in leadership. As a result of my ministry, my children were suffering from harassment. For example, when my daughter was five, they told her, "Your mother doesn't love you" because I was preaching one weekend a month. Another time they said, "Your mother is a witch because she prays for the sick."

After one such terrible incident, I decided I was quitting the ministry, certain that's what I needed to do. When Mike came home from work, the minute he walked through the door, I pointed my finger at him and said, "Mike Jacobs, I am quitting the ministry."

At first, Mike just stood there in shock. Then he calmly set down his briefcase and said, "You are not." And I looked at him and said, "I am too!" He said, "You are not!" And I said, "I am too!" Can you believe that? In the end, he won, and I stayed in ministry. But because of the hurt that I felt and my love for my children, I could have easily made a wrong decision. I needed Mike as a sounding board to help keep me on track.

As you begin to work through how to hear God's voice, I encourage you to pray in this manner: "God, will you give me some people I can trust? Will you give me a pastor, an elder, a prayer group? People around me, a friend? An accountability group that can help me to know what I should do?"

You may be asking, "Those are great guidelines, Cindy, but how do these steps work in the grand scheme of things?" That's a really good question, so let me give you an example. A few years ago, I had been up studying since about three in the morning, and the next day I was heading off to a ministry event. I was going on about four hours' sleep and was really in need of prayer. My little sister called me and immediately kicked into prayer as I was driving down the road. She knew exactly the type of prayer and encouragement I needed because, over the years, we had developed resonance.

I have prayer partners who I call when I have a need, and they call me. It's been years since we started praying for each other, and now, because we know each other's hearts and minds, we have a "collective ear" to hear from the Shepherd regarding each other. You are not alone in your quest to hear the Father's voice—but you need people who will help you, and God will provide them for you if you ask.

As we finish this chapter, I want you to think about your own life. I want you to take a moment to write down some things that you would ask the Lord for. Maybe as I have talked to you, you're looking back on your life, and you are thinking, *I have been hurt.* Perhaps it was similar to how I was hurt during that time at my children's school, or maybe your wounds are much deeper (e.g., betrayal, trauma from abuse, a prodigal child, etc.). Maybe the wounds were self-inflicted, and you realize you made some big mistakes—perhaps you don't trust yourself to accurately hear from God. You think you can't hear His voice anymore—that the volume has been turned off due to your wrong choices.

This is sad because He wants you to hear His voice! He wants you to make good decisions. Maybe you're facing some big decisions right now. You know, life is not steady. Wouldn't it be wonderful if we never had to make an important decision, if everything was always perfect? Well, that type of perfection will only happen when we die and go to heaven, because life is by no means perfect. But we don't have to dwell on death, however, because He wants to give you life—His voice is real, His love is present, and He does offer hope.

Abba Father is beckoning to you. He sees your pain and grieves with you—for things that have been done to you and for things that you have done to others or yourself. There is hope and forgiveness and grace and love—and He wants you to hear it in the clear, comforting sound of His welcome whisper.

Notes

1. Cindy Jacobs, *Deliver Us from Evil*, (Ventura: Regal Books, 2001), 115.

2. Cindy Jacobs, *The Voice of God*, (Ventura: Regal Books, 1995), 79.

Chapter Three

The Purpose of Prophecy

proph·e·cy noun: a statement that something will happen in the future ... the function or vocation of a prophet; specifically: the inspired declaration of divine will and purpose

-MERRIAM WEBSTER DICTIONARY

If you are a new Christian, or have limited experience with hearing God's voice, it's important that we clearly define terms. One word I've been using interchangeably with the expression "hearing God's voice" is the word "prophecy." Prophecy is hearing from God and then being directed by the Holy Spirit to act upon what you've heard.

There are two types of prophecy: personal prophecy and corporate prophecy. As you can probably discern, a personal prophecy is meant for one person (one-to-one), while a corporate prophecy is given to a body (such as a congregation, ministry, city, etc.). For the purposes of this book, we will talk exclusively about personal prophecy; thus, when I use the word "prophecy," I am referring to the personal type. (If you would like to learn more about corporate prophecy, see 1 Corinthians 12-14 for an in-depth discussion of both types of prophecy. As well, I talk a good deal about personal and corporate prophecy in my book *The Voice of God*.)

Prophecy has two main components: foretelling and forthtelling. Foretelling has to do with the future, as in hearing from God about an event that will happen beyond this present moment. Forthtelling has to do with proclaiming truth, as in hearing God about a current (or future) situation. For example, you might be struggling with whether or not to pursue a relationship with a certain person, and God reveals to you that it isn't His will for your life. That is forthtelling, rather than foretelling.

This is a very simplified description of prophecy, and there are many components of the prophetic that I've touched on in other books (again, see *The Voice of God*) and teachings (search the Generals International website for further reading). My purpose here is not to go into a deep teaching or description of the multiple facets of prophecy. Rather, for the sake of this overview on hearing God's voice, let's keep moving and discuss the functions of prophecy.

The Three Major Functions of Prophecy

A key scripture that describes the uses or functions of prophecy is 1 Corinthians 14:3, which says, "But he who prophesies speaks edification and exhortation and comfort to men."

What does this mean? Let's break down this key scripture and look at each of the three main functions.

Edification

According to *Webster's Dictionary*, the word "edify" means "to build, establish; to instruct and improve especially in moral and religious knowledge: to uplift." In the Greek, the word "edification" is *oikidone*, which literally means, "to build a house." In other words, a house of God will be built up through the prophetic word.

A prophetic word should edify you; it should build you up. Does that mean that when God speaks, it is always easy to hear what He wants to say? No, not always. Think of what it takes to renovate an old house. If you have ever built a home or renovated an existing house, you know that the process can be slow, painful, and somewhat draining (to your body and pocketbook!).

You don't need to own a home to understand what it takes to build or fix up a house. If you are a fan of home renovation shows (as am I!), then you know about the process. The funny thing about renovation shows is that they typically only show the highlights. At the beginning, you see the decrepit kitchen stuck in the 70s, and then, poof!—by the end of the show, it has been transformed into a beautiful, modern kitchen with lots of light, beautiful tile flooring, and all-modern appliances. However, what you usually don't see through this "building up" process is the work it took to tear down the old cabinets, remove the sink and countertops, and the labor required to install all the modern features.

Spiritual edification is often like that: what we want is the wonderful prophetic word that tells us how great things are going to be in the future. Sometimes, though, for us to be spiritually mature enough to handle God's best for us, the Lord first has to take us through a "home renovation" of our own—tearing down spiritual walls, replacing old thought patterns with new ones, or bringing humility into hidden areas of pride. This is still a process of "building up" (or edification); it just might not be as painless as you thought it would be.

If God's going to say something to you, it's going to be something that builds up your inner person, even if it's a corrective word. If the prophecy is said through the love of God, and it is biblical, it will build you up and not tear you down.

I remember one time my husband had a dream in which Jesus was rebuking a group of terrorists. He was telling them the evil things they were doing and rebuking their terrorism, but He said it with much love and kindness. And because of His compassion, the terrorists in the dream were totally broken by the love of God.

God's Word says His kindness leads to repentance (see Romans 2:4). Similarly, a prophetic word should be said with the love of Christ. And if it is, it will edify. However, if you have bitterness in your heart toward a person, you are not the right one to offer the word until your heart becomes clean. Not only do you have the responsibility to give the word, but you also have the responsibility to give the word in a way that's edifying.

What does a godly prophetic word do? It builds a house—it builds up your relationship with the Lord. Not only that, but if you hear the Lord and act upon His words in the right way, the ability to give and receive the prophetic will actually be transformational. Psalm 33:9 declares that God spoke, and the world came into being. And so it is with the prophetic voice of God—He creates words for His children, and we are edified by those words. There is something in God-filled words that changes a person's heart.

I remember years ago when I began to prophesy that it was time for local churches to begin developing freedom—or deliverance—ministries. The idea we have in our heads about deliverance often comes from Hollywood—including horror films where demons make people do terrible things, etc. But the vast majority of the time, deliverance is a quiet, positive process through which an individual is set free from sins of the past.

Yes, on occasion, there can be demonic manifestation (e.g., coughing, choking, strange sounds, falling on the floor, etc.), but through the power of the Holy Spirit, these situations can turn into examples of victory for God's kingdom. (Again, the purpose here is not to delve into deliverance—I speak about that subject at length in my book *Deliver Us From Evil*, if you are looking for further reading.)

Prior to God giving me that word of edification for the church, very few churches had deliverance ministries. Today, however, thousands of people are being set free from bad habits, hurts from the past, and sinful patterns through locally based deliverance ministries.

In the 80s, God encouraged me to prophesy that He wanted prayer groups to spread across the nation and world. That may sound strange to us today because it seems nearly all churches have some kind of organized prayer ministry or group. But in the mid-80s, when God gave me that prophetic word, very few churches had a prayer group. Today it's actually more unusual for a church not to have a prayer group or ministry. In fact, we have whole houses of prayer and 24-hour prayer houses now, but at one time, it was very hard to find a prayer group.

When I was writing my first book, *Possessing the Gates of the Enemy* in 1989, I tried to find material on intercessory prayer but only found one book. In case you are unfamiliar with the term, intercessory prayer has to do with "standing in the gap" for another person, situation, or event. In Ezekiel 22:30, God laments to the prophet Ezekiel, "I sought for a man among them who would make a wall, and stand in the gap before Me on behalf of the land, that I should not destroy it; but I found no one."

Today, God calls us to stand in the gap spiritually, to offer our prayers to Him on behalf of others. In this way, intercessory prayer is different from petitional prayer; rather than simply praying for our own circumstances, we are called to pray for others. God revealed to me that He wanted the church to more deeply enter into intercession, including prayer for cities and entire nations.

At that time, other prophets and I began to coin terms to express the things that intercessors had been doing for a long time but that the wider church was just learning about. For example, God led us to coin terms such as "prophetic prayer" and "intercessory worship." God used the prophetic realm to educate and edify His church.

With every new move of God, He will anoint people to speak prophetically to His church in order to uplift and edify. New phrases will be coined. There is no new truth, as the Word of God does not change or waver; however, there is restored truth —biblical truths that become forgotten or underused. Why are such seasons of restoration needed? Again, the Bible gives us the clear answer: "for the equipping of the saints for the work of ministry, *for the edifying of the body of Christ*" (Ephesians 4:12, emphasis mine).

Exhortation

The second major function of prophecy is exhortation. Webster's defines "exhort" as "to try to influence (someone) by words or advice: to strongly urge." In the Greek, exhort is translated *parakaleó*. You might recognize that word if you know a little bit of Greek. It also means paraclete or "helper" and, in Scripture, often refers to the Holy Spirit. The word exhortation can mean to encourage and help. God will give a word of exhortation in order for a person to be uplifted and encouraged in their walk. It is a type of prophetic word but different from edification.

Now let me explain this. Recently I was speaking at my home church in Dallas, Texas, and I sensed the Lord had a word of exhortation that He wanted me to give to the church. I then went to our pastor and told him I had an exhortation to give the congregation. I didn't say, "I have a prophecy." Why? Because I knew that what God wanted to share was not as much forthtelling or foretelling as it was a word that would bring them to a place of joy and hope.

You see, Satan wants to bring hopelessness into people's lives, but the prophetic word builds you up. It brings you hope; it exhorts you. It says, "Look, you're here! But don't stay there. You don't have to stay there because I am doing this."

When we think about the word of the Lord, let God use exhortation to build up His church. I love people with the spiritual gift of exhortation—they are such nice people! You know, other people see the negative in life, while they see the positive. When you are down, they are the ones who say, "Oh, I just know you can make it, and God is going to help you." Their nature is to encourage you. Why? It's because they are exhorters, and they are always going to be used by God to uplift and encourage.

Like edification, however, exhortation is not simply about encouragement; at times, we may be stuck in a place that is not where God wants us. When we are in the valley, God doesn't want us to remain there—exhortation can be a tool to encourage someone to not remain comfortable living in the wilderness. It can be a way for God to steer us away from traps, snares, and roadblocks that keep us from fulfilling our calling (or destiny).

Thus, there is a conviction and correction component to exhortation. But as with all things of God, the purpose of exhortation is not to heap guilt upon someone's head, but rather to lift up their head so they can see the vista in the distance—the place where God wants them to go.

Comfort

The third function of prophecy that we see in 1 Corinthians 14:3 is comfort. In the Greek, "to comfort or soothe" is translated as *parégoria*. Comforting and exhorting are similar prophetic functions, but there is a slight difference. When we exhort someone, there can be a convicting component, especially when the person needs to realize that God has a better plan for him or her. With the function of comforting, on the other hand, the purpose is always to soothe and bring peace—to offer the "balm of Gilead" no matter where a person is in their walk with God (see Jeremiah 8:22).

One of my favorite scriptures is 2 Corinthians 1:3:

> Blessed be the God of our Lord Jesus Christ, the Father of mercies and God of all comfort, who comforts us in all our tribulation, that we be able to comfort those who are in any trouble, with the comfort with which we ourselves are comforted by God.

Many times, when I am mentoring young leaders, I will say to them, "When you prophesy, ask God to speak right to the wilderness of that person's soul."

As God leads you to bring comfort to someone, ask Him, "If I could hear one thing from You, God, what do You want me to share with this person?" More often than not, the thing God brings to your mind will be the one particular issue that has been weighing heavily upon them.

As you ask God to give you the "balm of Gilead" for that person—the exact words of much-needed comfort—He will provide you with the precise wording. Oftentimes, the person to whom you are giving prophetic comfort will say something like, "How did you know that? Only God could know what you've just shared with me, and because of your prophetic words of comfort, I know there's a God in heaven who loves me."

Most of the time, the prophetic function of comfort will be straightforward and simple, such as discerning a person's pain and giving them scriptures that bring solace and peace to the heart. At other times, however, the prophecy might be a bit strange—at least to us (but not to God).

For example, some time ago I was ministering in Phoenix, Arizona, and a woman came to the altar and stood before me, awaiting prayer. I looked at her, and the next thing I knew I was singing the children's nursery rhyme "Twinkle, Twinkle, Little Star." It was quite strange, and as the words flew out of my mouth, I was thinking, *I am losing my mind. I'm either going crazy or I'm just overly tired!*

There I was, standing in front of a lot of people seeking ministry, and I was singing "Twinkle, twinkle, little star, how I wonder what you are. Up above the world so high, like a diamond in the sky!" And then suddenly, God gave me a word of comfort for this woman, and I said, "God is going to use you to bring joy to children."

She began to cry, and after she had composed herself, I asked her if my strange little performance had meant anything to her. She smiled broadly and said, "Yes! I've just started a children's entertainment ministry with my best friend, and we often sing 'Twinkle, Twinkle Little Star' to the children." You see, she had been praying, *Lord, please help me. I just need know we're doing the right thing.* She and her partner had put a lot of time and money into their ministry, and God knew that she needed to be comforted in a very specific way.

Let the Holy Spirit lead you to comfort people He puts in your path each day. Lean into the Holy Spirit, and ask Him to show you just what each particular person needs. If you pray for someone, don't just say, "God bless so and so." If the person has had a loss, ask God to show you how they feel, and identify with that, just as Jesus identifies with our pain. The more we identify with another person's sorrow, the more God will speak to us using the prophetic function of comfort. As always, Christ is our perfect example of how to enter into another person's sorrow and minister to them.

For example, on two occasions, the New Testament tells us that Jesus Himself wept. In one instance, He wept for the loss of a good friend (at the death of Lazarus; see John 11). In Hebrews 5:7, it says, "Jesus, who, in the days of His flesh, when He had offered up prayers and supplications, with vehement cries and tears to Him who was able to save Him from death, and was heard because of His godly fear."

There are other references that speak of Jesus lamenting (grieving, in pain) over a situation, such as right after His triumphal entry into the city of Jerusalem (see Matthew 21). He knows that His crucifixion is just days away, yet Jesus yearns to comfort His countrymen—if only they would allow Him to. In Matthew 23, He cries:

> O Jerusalem, Jerusalem, the one who kills the prophets and stones those who are sent to her! How often I wanted to gather your children together, as a hen gathers her chicks under her wings, but you were not willing! See! Your house is left to you desolate; for I say to you, you shall see Me no more till you say, "Blessed is He who

comes in the name of the Lord!"

MATTHEW 23: 30-39

Even though the majority of his fellow Jews have not received Him as the Messiah, He nonetheless grieves for them, revealing His desire to comfort them like a "hen gathers her chicks under her wings."

Jesus was the great Comforter, such as when He had mercy on the woman at the well (see John 4), and when He stood up to the teachers and Pharisees in the case of the woman accused of adultery (see John 8). In these examples, and numerous others in the Bible, Christ identified with the predicaments of those around Him and provided comfort and compassion.

Not only did Jesus identify with our pain when He allowed Himself to be placed on the cross to die for our transgressions, but He still identifies with our pain today. Like Christ, become a prophetic agent of God's comfort to others.

Chapter Four
Heal Your Past to Hear God in the Present

I grew up poor.

I mean, my family was really poor. The good thing is, we learned to pray to eat; to this day, I have great faith for food! This was the early 1950s in North Texas, and my daddy was in seminary. There wasn't a whole lot of extra money floating around our house at that time. My dad worked nights to pay for seminary, and my mom stayed home to raise my brother, sister and me.

I remember one day we didn't have any food on the table, so we began to pray for provision. Then, something unfortunate happened: the washing machine broke down. Now, not only did we not have food, but we were also looking at the possibility of hand-washing our clothes.

My daddy set his mind to fixing the broken machine. And you have to understand, my dad could fix anything; he had a lot of practice since there was never money to pay someone else to do the repairs. He started pushing that washing machine away from the wall. But you see, the floorboards in our house were warped and crooked—kind of like the house itself, which even leaned a little. To give you a more accurate idea of the condition of the house at the time—it was condemned and torn down after we moved out. It was one of those houses where you think, *one good wind and this house is going down.*

Well, out came the washing machine, my dad huffing and struggling to get the legs clear of the warped floorboards. As he finished clearing it away from the wall, we spotted something green and wet on the floor. At first I didn't want to look—I mean, I really didn't want to stare at something wet and green that had been living in the dark under our old washing machine!

Then we all saw what it was: a wet ten-dollar bill. Ten dollars was a lot back in those days, so we loaded up our old car and drove to the local supermarket, rejoicing as we bought our food. I'm sure the checkout lady wondered why a smelly, wet dollar bill was coming into her cash register, but who cares? We had food to eat!

To this day I thank God for that lesson of His provision: what seemed like a terrible thing—no food on the table and a broken washing machine—wasn't terrible at all. God had worked it out for us to eat that night.

You may be asking, "Cindy, that's a great story, but what does that have to do with the fact that I want to hear God—but can't. I believe He speaks, but I have no idea how to tune into His frequency." Great question. At the same time that my family was struggling in the midst of life's circumstances, God was speaking to me—a barefoot Texas girl living in a crooked house with a broken washing machine. And I knew, even then, that I had a choice: I could pursue Him, or I could let the difficulties of my life drown out His voice. And you have the same choice to open your heart to hear Him, or let life drown out his voice.

Due to the faith and example of my parents, I learned to believe the Word of God—that I could be in health and prosper. Despite a lack of financial wealth, we were a close family, and my parents loved us dearly.

Perhaps your circumstances are much worse than mine. Maybe you are in the midst of divorce, or grieving the pain of a prodigal child, or staring at the possibility of bankruptcy or unemployment. You may be asking: "God, do You really still speak today? Can I hear Your voice even in the midst of my difficulties and pain?"

The answer, my friend, is a resounding yes; however, sometimes like bad traffic on a Friday afternoon, there's a lot of clutter slowing us down, keeping us from our destination. In terms of better hearing from God, sometimes our lives fill with "traffic congestion"—past wounds, regrets, and experiences that drown out the voice of the Lord.

In this chapter, I want to explore some of the wounds and strongholds that can stop us from hearing God clearly and offer suggestions on how we can overcome these roadblocks.

Shipwrecked

Some people get shipwrecked in their hearts. They may prosper according to the world's definition, but in their hearts, they remain poor. When a person is shipwrecked, it's more difficult to hear God's voice. Let's say a person has the spiritual gift of giving. When they are shipwrecked, their ability to give might be stymied. Though God may want them to give, they're stuck, and so their strength has become their stronghold (or area of weakness and bondage). It's interesting, because oftentimes Satan wants to wound us in our places of greatest strength, not the areas of greatest weakness. If the enemy can successfully hinder our areas of greatest strength, then he has our destiny, doesn't he?

Paul understood this when he wrote to Timothy, one of his spiritual sons, and admonished him, saying, "Timothy, my son, I am giving you this command in keeping with the prophecies once made about you, so that by recalling them you may fight the battle well, holding on to faith and a good conscience, which some have rejected and so have suffered shipwreck with regard to the faith" (1 Timothy 1:18-19).

How about you? Do you feel spiritually shipwrecked in your life? Are you being tossed by circumstances, in the midst of the storm, barely keeping your head above water? Perhaps Apostle Paul's reference in 1 Timothy to being shipwrecked is no coincidence, as he, himself, had once been shipwrecked—literally.

In Acts 21, while aboard a ship en route to Rome to await trial before the emperor, a major storm overcame Paul's vessel, and all seemed lost. The Lord told Paul that not only would he survive, but that each and every person on the boat would survive too. And they did, running aground on the island of Malta and making it safely ashore.

Unfortunately, many people stay stranded on the rocks of misfortune and heartache. Oftentimes unresolved hurts, wounds, or traumas can keep a person impoverished on the inside, even though they might look "wealthy and healthy" on the outside. Now, I know some of you reading this have been through terrible things that no person should have to endure. I am not saying your wounds are not real, or that you just need to "believe" more to move out of the place you are in.

Becoming spiritually shipwrecked is often a subtle process, slowly happening over time. Maybe you were abandoned physically or emotionally, or maybe you lost everything you have in life—financially and relationally. Now you have run aground spiritually; you don't believe God is good, and you don't believe life will ever be better than it was before. Or maybe you don't trust anymore.

One of the things God has spoken to us is that we need to have great expectations. Maybe you don't have expectations anymore, and your life is defined by your shipwrecks. Or perhaps you experienced a moral failure—something for which you've repented, but you still have an imaginary slash across your chest that reads like a scarlet letter "A." If you do, it's time to take it off! Remove the letter and determine that you are a new creation in Christ (see 2 Corinthians 5:17); recognize that Jesus loves you so much that He went to the cross for your moral failures (see 1 Peter 2:24). Be assured that He does have a plan for your life, even when you have seriously made a mistake—because everybody has.

Even the most experienced, godly leaders make mistakes. But the vast majority of God's warriors learn that they can get up from their mistakes, clean up what they can, and trust God with the rest.

I don't want to underestimate the pain you might be in as you read this. Being betrayed by the ones you love the most can be the most painful experience on earth. Maybe that is what happened to cause you to shipwreck. From that day of betrayal, perhaps you turned away from God's calling and never pursued what He wanted you to do. How sad is that? You see, "the gifts and callings of God are without repentance" (Romans 11:29, KJV). In the NKJV, the verse reads "the gifts and calling of God are irrevocable." In other words, when God calls you, He means to do something—He wants to use you. It comes down to choices. Are you going to choose to stay shipwrecked?

Author and world prayer leader Dr. C. Peter Wagner is my mentor, and one of the things I admire most about Peter is his constant willingness to learn, grow, and seek the wisdom of other people (even as an 80-something-year-old believer!). And Peter doesn't stay stuck—when he makes a mistake, he repents, cleans up the mess the best he can, and surrenders the rest to God. How refreshing and encouraging!

My hope and prayer is that God is going to "unstick" you. Maybe someone violated you in some way, which is a horrific thing. Or, perhaps you had an abortion. Though you may have a great deal of pain from that experience, God can use you to speak words of encouragement and healing to other women grieving their own abortions.

One sign that you've been shipwrecked is when you stop growing spiritually in a certain area. Many people prophesy and make a mistake, so they never prophesy again. That is tragic because if you're called to prophesy, you have to learn. That is what grace and mercy are all about: receiving God's permission to try, fail, and then get up and try again.

Inner Vows

An inner vow is a decision you make, either consciously or unconsciously, in a moment of pain or trauma.

For example, perhaps a pastor hurt you and as a result, you made a vow: "I will never trust a pastor again." Or you might have been hurt through a relationship and you vowed, "I will never let anyone get emotionally close to me again." So many times, people don't make a conscious decision to make an inner vow, but they make them nonetheless. And out of the seed of that inner vow grows a harvest of "I will nevers": "I will never love again"; "I will never trust again"; "I will never minister again . . ."

Stop for a moment and reflect through prayer: are there any inner vows that the Lord is revealing to you? If so, surrender them at His altar—yes, we are all living sacrifices, and as such, we tend to crawl off the altar! And that's okay; you may not be able to lay that vow down instantly. It may take time. Don't give up, and don't try to do it in your own power.

If you have a trusted brother or sister in Christ, take them into your confidence, and ask for their prayer support and accountability. The simple but bold act of reaching out for help and risking the trust of another person can be, in itself, a part of the breaking of that inner vow. Remember that the purpose of this book is to help you hear God more clearly. By recognizing and surrendering your inner vows, you begin the process toward having "ears to hear" God more clearly (see Mark 4:9).

How do you break an inner vow? First of all, ask the Holy Spirit to show you what those inner vows are. When you enter into this process to consciously pursue God in the breaking of inner vows, He will begin to reveal them to you.

Next, make a list of the things the Lord reveals to you. And again, if you do know another believer whom you can trust, have them pray for you as well. How have you become shipwrecked? In the oceans upon which you have sailed in life, where are those hidden shoals—those dangerous rocky graveyards where you have run aground?

Sometimes it takes a little time to hear from the Lord regarding your inner vows. That is because we humans are very good at something called denial. We think we are just fine and that there's nothing really wrong with us. But deep down, we know it isn't true.

Once you compile your list (it could be quite short, or it could be quite long, which is okay), enter a place of quiet prayer. You might want to say, "Father God, I now renounce this vow in the name of Jesus, and I pray that You free me from it. Break its power over me." And then you pray the opposite: "Now, Lord, the truth is I choose to be in faith over . . ." In other words, you embrace the godly opposite of your inner vow, which comes in the form of a biblical promise.

For example, let's say as a child you were abandoned by a parent, so you have made an inner vow to never again trust an authority figure. Seek out verses that affirm God's love for you, such as Deuteronomy 31:6: "Be strong and of good courage, do not fear nor be afraid of them; for the Lord your God, He is the One who goes with you. He will not leave you nor forsake you." Soak in God's Word, "for it is living and powerful, and sharper than any two-edged sword, piercing even to the division of soul and spirit, and of joints and marrow, and is a discerner of the thoughts and intents of the heart"

(Hebrews 4:12). Take your list, and for every negative vow, make a list of scriptures that are the opposite of that vow (such as the preceding examples from Deuteronomy and Hebrews).

As you exchange Satan's lies (i.e., your inner vows) with God's truth, you will be able to more freely choose to be in faith and walk out of those debilitating vows that stop you from hearing God with the clarity, accuracy, and intimacy that He desires for you.

An inner vow is a very powerful spiritual pact that we unwittingly make with ourselves. It's like a wrongfully made covenant that needs to be broken. Ask the Holy Spirit to heal you, and remember that whatever we ask we receive from Him (1 John 3:22). Give your expectations to God. Take time for Him to heal you, and as you do, the path toward hearing God will open up before you.

Disappointments

I have found that in my own life, one of the biggest impediments to hearing God is disappointment.

I recently wrote the following in a time of reflection: "How we deal with past failures and mistakes will determine how we are able to hear God more clearly in the future." The thing is, we all make mistakes; not one of us is perfect.

Maybe you are nearly perfect, but I am certainly not anywhere close! Just ask my friends (or better yet, my husband and kids). For one reason or another, everyone has had a time where they didn't accurately discern the will of God for their lives. For some people, "missing God" can be a crippling experience with lasting negative repercussions. They make a mistake or believe they've heard God's will, only to "miss it" completely. Thus, they become paralyzed.

Disappointment then becomes the ugly twin brother of an inner vow. One always goes with the other. But as we discussed above, when we allow past wounds and disappointments to paralyze us, we have already conceded victory to the enemy. He has won—because if he can knock us off course from our destiny, he has successfully scuttled God's plan for our lives. The hardest thing to do in life is to fight when we don't feel like fighting. You know those times where it feels like all your emotional and spiritual energy has just been sucked right out of you—and you have nothing left? How do you fight when you have no fight left in you?

There is a wonderful verse in Exodus that I turn to when I feel depleted from disappointments. In Exodus 14, the Israelites have finally shaken off the shackles of slavery and are in the midst of their escape from Pharaoh. They are literally between a rock and a hard place, encamped with the sea on one side and the wrath of Pharaoh on the other. Do you think they might have felt a bit disappointed? Yeah, me too!

It is there, prior to when God performed the wonder of parting the Red Sea, that "Moses said to the people, 'Do not be afraid. Stand still, and see the salvation of the Lord, which He will accomplish for you today. For the Egyptians whom you see today, you shall see again no more forever. The Lord will fight for you, and you shall hold your peace'" (Exodus 14:13-14). I love what the NIV says: "and you need only be still."

The New Living Translation says, "Just stay calm." More than a catchy slogan on a coffee mug, this is nitty-gritty, real-life stuff. Would you be able to "just stay calm" if you had the iron-rimmed wheels of 600 war chariots thundering in your ears, ready to grind you and your loved ones into the Egyptian dust? (Me neither.) How absurd! But that is the level of trust into which God is calling us to partake.

And the whole point is this: In our own power, shrugging off heavy burdens and disappointments can be impossible sometimes. But with God, all things are possible (see Matthew 19:26). Do you see the beauty here? God is yearning to reach down, gently take hold of your wounds and disappointments, and surgically remove them from your heart. Will the surgery leave a scar? Undoubtedly—and perhaps a big one. But God loves to use your scars as a testimony of His healing; in order to heal, sometimes we first need to be cut by the Holy Spirit's steady, loving hand.

One of the most powerful Old Testament prophecies regarding the coming Christ can be found in the book of Isaiah. Verse 53:5 says, "But He was wounded for our transgressions, He was bruised for our iniquities; the chastisement for our peace was upon Him, and by His stripes we are healed." Scholars estimate the prophet Isaiah penned these words around 700 BC—more than seven centuries before the crucifixion of Jesus. Isn't that amazing?

But what is more amazing is that in Luke 22:37, Jesus says that He is "numbered with the transgressors" (in this context, Jesus is referencing a prophecy about Himself, also found in Isaiah 53, verse 12). What we learn—and how we can be encouraged in the midst of gut-wrenching disappointments—is that Jesus can relate to our problems. But Jesus more than relates—He experiences what we experience; He numbers Himself amongst us and understands what it means to suffer. In essence, He "takes on" our disappointments and counts Himself amongst us (the transgressors). This does not mean that Jesus was a sinner; it means that He willingly took on the sins of the world that we might have eternal life.

"Cindy, what does this have to do with the fact that my son is addicted to drugs, I'm unemployed, and my COBRA insurance just expired, so I can't afford rehab for my child?" Beloved one, it has everything to do with the terrible disappointments and anguish you might be experiencing. You see, God knew that, alone, we wouldn't be able to handle the problems of this world. (As an aside, if you ever meet someone who says they don't have any problems, don't buy it. They are either lying or in heavy denial). Jesus' admonition is that we don't have to carry our burdens alone; He will be our helper, our comforter—but even more, He will be our deliverer.

If you are a student of the Bible, you've probably heard people misquote Matthew 11:29. The verse doesn't say that Jesus will take the yoke (burdens of life) away from us. He says, "*Take My yoke upon you* and learn from Me, for I am gentle and lowly in heart, and you will find rest for your souls*" (emphasis mine). Jesus is saying that when we take up His yoke (enter into relationship with Him and surrender our troubles to Him), He will give us rest for our weary souls. It may not happen overnight, and it might not mean that all your disappointments disappear instantly (it is, after all, still a yoke—or harness). It is a process—but you are not alone in carrying the burden.

Forgiving Yourself

If disappointment is the ugly brother of an inner vow, then forgiving yourself is the healing balm for both, given to us through the power of the Holy Spirit. Intellectually, most of us understand that through Christ, we are forgiven of our sins. We also can agree that God forgives us when we repent of our sins. But then, upon this highway called forgiveness, we see a much less traveled, narrow road: the sign says it is the road toward forgiveness of self.

Why is it so hard for us to take this more lightly traversed road along the highway of forgiveness? Because we are typically harder on ourselves than we are on others. We gladly receive salvation and the forgiveness of our sins yet have a hard time forgiving ourselves for the same sins God so readily forgives! It's mystifying, in a way; we accept that God forgives us, yet we harbor unforgiveness within our hearts toward ourselves (and, at times, others).

Hear me carefully because I don't want you to misunderstand: when we fail to forgive ourselves after God has forgiven us, we cheapen the gift of the Cross. As we enter into relationship with Christ, He takes away all our sins and casts them as far as the east is from the west (see Psalm 103:12). In doing so, His grace also covers our feelings of failure and self-loathing for what we have done. It is not just an external forgiveness; it is internal—He has forgiven us, thus He will also give us the grace to forgive ourselves.

When we accept His justification (i.e., when God makes us righteous through the forgiveness of sins when we choose to follow Christ), we must also accept His sanctification—wherein we are set aside for the lifelong purpose of becoming more like Christ. A major part of this process is allowing His grace to reach down to the darkest places of unforgiveness in your own heart. As you do, you will be able to hear His loving voice more clearly.

Sometimes we just have to say to ourselves, "Get up out of your failure mode!" Make a decision today that you can hear God's voice. Realize that even though you made a mistake, you can decide that your life is greater than that one bad choice. Maybe your decision had a major impact—such as deciding to pursue divorce or walk away from an important commitment. Even still, do we embrace Romans 8:28? Do we truly believe that all things work together for good for those who love the Lord and are called according to His purpose?

Many times, even when I make a mistake, I say, "Alright, God, I've missed Plan A. But I'm not going to miss Plan B." Do you understand this? It's saying to oneself, "I'm going to do it better next time. I'm going to take what I've learned from my failure, and I am going to go forward."

"Ah, Cindy," you might be saying. "If only it were that easy." Okay, I get it: reading a book won't necessarily fix your unforgiveness problem. You feel utterly stuck—perhaps you have even thought about suicide. You've reached a place where you cannot go on; you're paralyzed, and you're always looking backward, unable to even think about looking forward.

What does that say? Dear one, it says that in your heart, you do not believe that all things work together for good. If that is where you are, then ask the Lord to help your unbelief. Willing yourself—in your own power—to believe can be just one more disappointment heaped upon a pile of other disappointments. Belief is a supernatural process that is forged through the natural circumstances of living daily in Christ—in learning each day that God is greater than we are, knows more than we do, and has a better plan for us than we could ever conjure up. It's not like we can all count to three and suddenly be full of belief! Instead, ask God to meet you where you are, with whatever level of belief you possess. Trust me, the Lord will meet you there and even surprise you as you choose to lean into Him, turning your unforgiveness over to Him.

Here is something actionable I do when something bad happens to me, and I might be wrestling with guilt or unforgiveness. I say out loud, "The truth is, the devil is not going to stop this from working for my good. The truth is, this is not the end of this story. The truth is—right now, Father God—You are working everything for my good. I believe that in this moment You are moving heaven and earth because I am Your beloved child, and You are going to help. Things are going to work out better for me, and one day this test will be a testimony. One day, despite all the horrible things that have happened to me, I'm going to say, 'You know, I made a mistake. But now I am here at this point, and look how it has worked for my good.'"

Take a chance—just a baby step. If you are able to do that, it is a start. Remember, God does not despise small beginnings (see Zechariah 4:10).

Chapter Five

Obstacles to Hearing God Clearly

Have you ever been to the Grand Canyon? If you haven't, then I'd highly recommend you put it on your "bucket list."

The two most popular ways to see the beauty of this "Natural Wonder of the World" are from the North Rim or the South Rim. Depending upon whom you talk to, there's an ongoing debate as to which Rim is better. I heard a story from a friend who was excited to see the Canyon from the North Rim, which is more remote, less crowded, and a little more difficult to get to.

My friend was excited about visiting the Grand Canyon for the very first time and had taken time to study the route to the North Rim. Upon arriving at the entrance of the road that leads to the North Rim, he and his family were confronted with a locked, abandoned gate blocking their path. A sign read, "North Rim Access Closed Until Spring."

What he didn't realize is that because of the higher elevations from the north side of the Canyon, the roads are sometimes closed in the late fall and don't reopen until the spring, after the snows melt. He was quite disappointed, even though he and his family were able to have a nice visit to the South Rim (which is amazingly beautiful as well).

Sometimes our goals get blocked, and we are not able to reach the "North Rims" in our life. It can also be like that with hearing God: our ability to reach our destination is blocked by gates and locks, which come in the form of adversities, wounds, and life's letdowns.

Similar to the last chapter, I want to continue to highlight some roadblocks that can keep us from hearing God more clearly. In doing so, pray that the Lord would lead you toward specific solutions that relate to your particular life circumstances.

Unmet Expectations

At one point in my life I was really feeling down, so I asked the Lord, "Why am I depressed?" I then heard the Lord say, "Your depression is frozen anger." I said, "What am I angry about?" The Lord said, "You had expectations in your life of the way things would happen, but they didn't go that way. You thought that by this age, certain things would have happened, and you would have been in a different place financially. So, you are upset."

I thought about family members and things I thought should have happened with them. I also thought about goals and ambitions I had set for myself, and because I had not accomplished them, I was upset. In order to tackle my anger, I made a list of these unmet expectations. As I reviewed the list, I realized there were some things I couldn't change. For many items, I understood that other people had made those decisions for me. These experiences had affected my family and me, yet there was nothing I could do about them. But I could give them to God. I wrote down my frustrations as a way to surrender them to God.

One of my biggest unmet expectations had to do with my father, who died very suddenly at 49. As you can imagine, it deeply affected my whole family. My brother and sister were especially affected, and my little sister went away from the Lord for many years. (Later, I am happy to say, she did come back to God, stronger than before.) But at the time, I was quite upset about that. I was thinking, *Lord, we were raised in a Christian family; how is it that my sister can be like this?*

And you know, sometimes I had to get away from everyone and everything and just weep and mourn about the double loss of my deceased dad and my prodigal sister. Those times of crying and grieving were so healing, and sometimes the tears would flow for days. Through this period, I kept a journal in my Bible and would re-read my entries over and over.

Disobedience

Disobedience can get in the way of a person hearing from God or from a prophetic word coming to pass. For example, I remember giving a prophetic word to a couple that went something close to this: "The Lord says, 'I'm going to give you a better job and then a house,'" and then the prophecy continued with many more specifics.

Soon afterward, even though neither of them had yet found a job, they borrowed money and bought a house. Predictably, with no source of income, they soon lost the home. They contacted me and were very upset that "the prophecy did not come true." I urged them to go back and listen to the prophetic word again (at that time we captured the words on tape). I said, "Look, the prophecy said you would secure a job, so you could then pay for a house—not the other way around." In essence, they were in disobedience to the word the Lord had given them—that is also called living in presumption.

This is why I like to have prophesies recorded because sometimes you give a prophecy, and you don't record it, and then people blame you, thinking you messed up their lives! However, the key point is that disobedience is a serious issue that can severely impede our ability to hear clearly from the Lord. Perhaps one of the most dramatic cases of disobedience mixed with presumption is found in Acts 5 and involves Ananias and his wife, Sapphira, who were members of the church at Jerusalem.

They sell a plot of land and rather than give all the proceeds to the church as they said they had, they secretly hold back some of the money for themselves. Because of their disobedience, God actually strikes them dead! The interesting piece of this story is found in Acts 5:3, after the Holy Spirit reveals to the apostle Peter that the couple has deceived the church. Peter says, "Ananias, why has Satan filled your heart to lie to the Holy Spirit and keep back part of the price of the land for yourself?"

When we are in disobedience, we can't hear clearly from God. Instead, like Ananias and his wife, we are at risk of lying to the Holy Spirit and having our heart filled with deception and disobedience.

Sin

Sometimes God will not give a redemptive word if you're in sin. It's an enigma because we are all sinners, and if a complete lack of sin were the prerequisite for hearing from God, then such clarity would be reserved exclusively for Jesus, the only sinless person to ever walk the earth.

But think about this: Oftentimes, the fulfillment of a prophetic word is only found through the surrendering of a certain sin or thought pattern. In other words, in order for God to bring about the reality of what He has said to you, He first needs to deal with a specific problem or sin in your life.

We see a perfect example of this in John 4, when Jesus is traveling from Judea to Galilee via Samaria, a land deemed unclean by the Jews. John 4:3-4 says, "He left Judea and departed again to Galilee. But He needed to go through Samaria." Yes, cutting through Samaria was the shortest route between these two places, but the verse could also be suggesting that Jesus was led by God to go through this land of non-Jews.

Either way, His journey takes Him to Jacob's well in the town of Sychar where He stops for a drink along the dusty road. It is there that He meets a Samaritan woman:

> A woman of Samaria came to draw water. Jesus said to her, "Give Me a drink." For His disciples had gone away into the city to buy food. Then the woman of Samaria said to Him, "How is it that You, being a Jew, ask a drink from me, a Samaritan woman?" For Jews have no dealings with Samaritans. Jesus answered and said to her, "If you knew the gift of God, and who it is who says to you, 'Give Me a drink,' you would have asked Him, and He would have given you living water." The woman said to Him, "Sir, You have nothing to draw with, and the well is deep. Where then do You get that living water? Are You greater than our father Jacob, who gave us the well, and drank from it himself, as well as his sons and his livestock?" Jesus answered and said to her, "Whoever drinks of this water will thirst again, but whoever drinks of the water that I

shall give him will never thirst. But the water that I shall give him will become in him a fountain of water springing up into everlasting life." The woman said to Him, "Sir, give me this water, that I may not thirst, nor come here to draw." Jesus said to her, "Go, call your husband, and come here." The woman answered and said, "I have no husband." Jesus said to her, "You have well said, 'I have no husband,' for you have had five husbands, and the one whom you now have is not your husband; in that you spoke truly."

JOHN 4:7-18

In this powerful story of redemption, the Samaritan woman found God's true living water through the prophetic words of Christ—who already knew she was living in sin, even before she told Him. In this instance, God needed to confront the Samaritan woman with her sin of adultery in order for her to repent of her past and move into her future.

Several years ago I was ministering at a conference, and at one point, several of the ministers began to pray for a man, telling him that he needed to be set free. But they weren't getting very far and couldn't grasp exactly how to set him free. I had been sitting off to the side and felt God tell me to approach the ministers—sort of like a sidebar, out of earshot of the man.

I said, "He's having an affair." (I can be a scary person sometimes!) I singled out one of the lead pastors and said, "You are never going to get that guy delivered; he's having an affair. Go ask him." Though they knew this man really well, they had no idea of any affair. But sure enough, when they asked him, he admitted that he was indeed having a sexual affair. I approached the man and said, "God just told me that you are having an affair," and the man literally turned white with shock. I said, "Are you ready to repent?" He said, "Yes." Then God set him totally free, and he immediately broke off the affair.

The purpose of the prophetic word was to prove to the man that God sees all and that He cared enough about that man to not allow him to continue messing up his destiny by living in adultery. Like the woman at the well, God needed to first confront the sin in that man's life in order for him to fully embrace the better path God had for him.

Unbelief

Consider the story in the book of Mark about the father whose son was afflicted by an unclean spirit. The father was desperate and pleaded with Jesus to help his tormented boy. We pick up the narrative in Mark 9: "Jesus said to him, 'If you can believe, all things are possible to him who believes.' Immediately the father of the child cried out and said with tears, 'Lord, I believe; help my unbelief!'" (Mark 9:23-24) Guess what? Like the common cold, unbelief affects virtually all of us at some time or another.

Sometimes, even though God is trying to show us that we can believe in Him, we just simply decide not to believe what heaven is trying to tell us. It's so important to mix what God says with the faith that we do possess—even if, like the father in Mark 9, our faith is faltering. As we mix our relatively puny faith with God's promises, amazing things can happen. Remember that even Jesus' apostles struggled with puny faith. Over and over in the Scriptures, Jesus encourages His followers to have more faith.

For example, in Luke 17, the apostles ask Jesus to increase their faith. In response, Christ says, "If you have faith as a mustard seed, you can say to this mulberry tree, 'Be pulled up by the roots and be planted in the sea,' and it would obey you" (Luke 17:6). If God has spoken to you prophetically—directly or through another person—then He wants that word or promise to be fulfilled. Does He expect you to conjure up that faith on your own? No. He will meet you where you are, through the power and ministry of the Holy Spirit.

Even though you may feel like a little mouse and the task God has laid out for you seems overwhelming and terrifying, God is a big God, and He is able to manifest Himself through you. Many times the Holy Spirit wants to do great things for us, but we just say, "I can't, I can't." That is when we need to trust that He will, indeed, catch us and guide us to fulfill that seemingly impossible task He's laid before us.

You say, "Is there something God cannot do?" Well, if He wants to use you and you refuse, He'll have to find another person to do it. Therefore, don't stay stuck in doubt and unbelief. And yes, that can be difficult! Personally, just when I think I no longer have doubt and unbelief, God will call me to do a new thing, and I'll realize I don't have the measure of faith to do it.

That is when I need to get before the Lord and admit that I don't yet have the measure of faith to do that new thing. I'll pray Hebrews 11 (the faith chapter), get up early to pray and meditate on the scriptures, and feed myself on faith. Why? Because I know that if I want to get to a new level of faith, I have to do battle in my own mind and emotions until I get to a place where I obtain the measure of faith that I need.

Remember that faith is "the substance of things hoped for, the evidence of things not seen" (Hebrews 11:1). Has God whispered to you about certain things He wants you to do? But do you then wonder how you are ever going to be able to do them? That is when you need to pray for the Holy Spirit to guide you and to ask God, "What do I need to do to get there? Give me strategy; show me how to do it."

To clarify, I am not talking about presumptive faith where we believe for the biggest yacht rather than Kingdom-building. God is interested in growing the character you need so you will know what to ask Him for. He is more interested in your heart than in your pocketbook. Does that mean some of you don't have the gift of finance or ability to create wealth? No. But it does mean that no matter what God sets before you to do, He will guide you and give you the plan to accomplish it. Our part is to step out and allow Him to "grow us" into the measure of faith proportionate with the ability needed to accomplish that task.

Unbelief creeps in before we even know it, doesn't it? Maybe you think you're undeserving or that you don't know how to do this particular task—but God knows how. God knows. And He knows how to get you to where you need to go.

Don't let doubt be your enemy. If someone gives you a prophetic word and you have unbelief, you need to set your mind and heart to conquering that unbelief. You can pray, "Lord, yes, I'm going to do it. I'm struggling with the measure of faith, but I know You will help me with my unbelief. Please show me how." And God will begin to bring circumstances into your life and arrange things for you so that the word will come true.

Bitterness

Bitterness will block the word of the Lord from coming true in your life. God might give you an amazing prophetic word, but until you deal with any sins of unforgiveness and bitterness, He's never going to let you go to the next level. (Ouch, that hit a nerve!) It's so critical to understand that the Lord is more interested in us walking in His character and nature than He is in what we accomplish in the world. His passion is for what we are on the inside, more than the "success" on the outside. As I shared before, He wants us to be successful in our character first.

In His pursuit to develop our character, God will put pressure to bear on our lives, so we begin to cry out to Him. He wants us to get to that point where we say, "Okay, Lord, what is blocking Your will?" Sometimes it is a character issue. On the other hand, sometimes God deals with people in their character, but they get comfortable only going halfway in His plan.

For example, Joseph's brothers were jealous of their father Jacob's favoritism toward their youngest brother, so they threw him in a pit and left him for dead. Do you think Joseph got comfortable living in that pit? How about you? Have you grown accustomed to your pit to the point where you've started to decorate it and get comfortable? Perhaps deep inside you think, *I'm just going to make my life a little bit better. I'm just going to be content where I am.* On the other hand, perhaps God gave you a prophetic word that He would "give you the nations for your inheritance" as an international speaker or missionary.

But now you are stuck in one place—your own comfortable pit. If so, you have to call off those interior decorators that are designing your pit. You have to get up out of there. You need to say, "Okay, God gave me a word, so I'm going to get out of this pit." As you face your unbelief, release it to God, and take the steps necessary in your own free will, He will meet you.

God knows!

Limited Thinking

Just like the pit we touched on in the previous section, there can also be a box in our thinking that prohibits us from following the will of God. We might have received a prophetic word that God was going to do great things with us, but we have this six-sided box—the four walls might be poverty, fear, insecurity, and addiction; the ceiling might be intimidation, and the floor might be loneliness.

There you are, stuck in a box crafted by the devil using raw materials salvaged from the unfortunate circumstances in your life. In order for the word of the Lord to come true, you have to get out of that box. How do you do that? First, it comes by making a willful decision to seek the Lord. Consider the words of Psalm 40, penned by King David who was stuck in his own sort of box:

> I waited patiently for the Lord;
>
> And He inclined to me,
>
> And heard my cry.
>
> He also brought me up out of a horrible pit,
>
> Out of the miry clay,
>
> And set my feet upon a rock,
>
> And established my steps.
>
> PSALM 40:1, 2

Of all the great prophets of the Old Testament, perhaps none struggled with pits and boxes as much as David. Yet, David didn't decorate his pit—he arose from it, not by his own strength, but by the strength of the Lord. You see, he "cried out to the Lord"—made a willful step toward getting out of his pit. And guess what? The Lord heard David's cry and "put a new song in his mouth" (v. 3).

As a young woman in the 1980s, God began to whisper many wonderful things to me about my life. At the time, I was bound by fear and intimidation, so I began to fast and pray. I said, "Lord, if there is in anything in me that is holding me back, I want You to change it. I don't want to be the one that stops Your will from coming to pass in my life." At that point, God began to show me amazing things, and I began to take those steps of faith that I desperately needed in order to break out of my own box.

Spiritual Warfare

As you grow in your ability to hear the Lord, you will inevitably encounter spiritual warfare. A simple description of spiritual warfare is interference from the enemy. I always chuckle when I hear the story of the man who was explaining to his son that Satan is real. The son was buying none of it and said, "I just don't believe in the devil!" In response, the father simply lowered his head a bit, looked into his son's eyes, and said, "Oh, don't worry about that, son, because the devil believes in you."

Clever stories aside, we do live in a world where there is evil and there is good. The Bible tells us that Satan roams the earth like a roaring lion, looking for those whom he can devour (see Job 1:7: 1 Peter 5:8). Does that mean we need to live in fear of the demonic realm? No. First of all, He who is in us is greater than he who is in the world; in other words, Christ is greater than Satan and his dark forces (see 1 John 4:4). Second, once for all Christ defeated Satan through His resurrection. Revelation 12:11 confirms this, saying, "And they overcame him [the devil] *by the blood of the Lamb* and by the word of their testimony, and they did not love their lives to the death" (emphasis mine).

When you feel pressed in by the enemy, press into prayer each day and ask others to pray for you. Solicit prayer from other brothers and sisters in Christ who will help "pray you through" the particular trial or tribulation you are enduring.

Consider fasting as a tool to break the strongholds of the enemy in your life. You could start with a simple one-meal fast, then slowly work your way up to two or three days. As well, there are many different types of fasts, such as fasting from sugar, television, solid foods (other than nutritional liquids), etc. Prior to beginning a fasting regimen, consult with your physician, especially if you struggle with health issues. Also, there are many wonderful books on fasting that I highly recommend, such as *Fasting for Spiritual Breakthrough* by Elmer Towns and *Fasting* by Jentezen Franklin.

The classic passage on spiritual warfare is Ephesians 6:11, which urges us to put on the full armor of God that we may be able to stand against the wiles of the devil. And what is the full armor? Paul makes it clear in his epistle to the church at Ephesus:

> Stand therefore, having girded your waist with truth, having put on the breastplate of righteousness, and having shod your feet with the preparation of the gospel of peace; above all, taking the shield of faith with which you will be able to quench all the fiery darts of the wicked one. And take the helmet of salvation, and the sword of the Spirit, which is the word of God; praying always with all prayer and supplication in the Spirit . . .
>
> EPHESIANS 6:14-18

Self-Deception

Sometimes I hear people say, "I don't listen to anybody because I already know the voice of God." For me, that's a big red flag. I like saying, "Oh dear, you're already self-deceived." You know, if you don't think you can be deceived, you already are. Anyone can be deceived, so that's why we need others around us to help us. God never created a vacuum of hearing; He purposely has a collective ear.

This is why the Bible says, "By the mouth of two or three witnesses every word shall be established." In this passage from 2 Corinthians 13:1, Paul is addressing the church at Corinth, known for its immaturity and spiritual struggles. Why do you think Paul says there should be "two or three witnesses"? It's because Paul understands that the Corinthians are not mature enough to hear God clearly by them-selves—they need each other to affirm, confirm, and test the word.

Don't be a spiritual lone ranger as you pursue the voice of God; make sure you surround yourselves with other growing, surrendered believers who are living by God's Word and pursuing Him through the power of the Holy Spirit.

I tell the story in my book *Possessing the Gates of the Enemy* how one day I received a telephone call from two women. As each took turns asking for prayer, each one began the conversation with, "God has told me that I'm going to marry [name of well-known evange-list]," who was single at the time. As I prayed with the first woman, I said, "Well, I don't have a prophetic word about that, but we'll ask the Lord." For the second woman I said, "God would not say this to both of you!" You know, this preacher is not going to have two wives, okay? We don't believe in that—polygamy is not appropriate for a good, Bible-believing, Jesus person!

I quickly realized there was some deception there, so I called each of them back and said, "Look, both of you feel the same thing. Are you willing to release this desire to the Lord and be willing to say, 'Lord, bring the right one to me'?" To their credit, both women agreed (and to the best of my knowledge, none of them married that evangelist).[3]

Loneliness

How can a person mishear the Lord so badly and become utterly self-deceived? One reason is out of loneliness. When we don't have a lot of people to talk to, life is hard, right? I have many single friends, and I really empathize with them because it's hard not having some-one to process with you. I will quickly add that some of my sin-gle friends are quite content being single and believe it to be God's plan for their lives. And of course, the Apostle Paul sets a very good biblical example of a spiritual hero whom most scholars believe remained single his entire life. But for many other single friends, they are hoping and praying for a spouse. At times, God will show you your spouse, and it will be the voice of God. In fact, I have just such a friend.

The first time author and speaker Dutch Sheets saw his future wife, Ceci, singing in a choir, he just knew he was going to marry her. Now, after more than 30 years of marriage, I tease Dutch and say, "I don't know if you should tell that story to young people because you're going to get everybody in trouble. They're all going to claim the same person!"

But in this case, Dutch was right. However, more importantly, Dutch knew how to hear the voice of God, and he heard clearly—it wasn't just a random emotion or passing infatuation. As well, Dutch didn't stop there—even though he believed God had told him he would marry Ceci, Dutch still prayed, sought God's Word, and pursued counsel to confirm the word. That is godly wisdom in action.

Years ago I was teaching for an Aglow International chapter in Waco, Texas, and this woman said, "God has told me I'm getting married." The Lord nudged my spirit though, as her statement didn't resonate with me (see more on "resonance" in Chapters 2 and 6). I asked, "Are you already married?" And she said, "Well, yes." I said, "Why do you need to get married if you're already married?" She responded, "Oh no, no . . . my husband is going to die."

As you can imagine, I was a bit shocked and said, "He's going to die?! Okay, and ma'am, you think you're hearing from God? How about the other man—is he married?" She replied, "Yes, but my prayer group has told me that because his wife is in rebellion to his call, that she's going to die, too."

At this point I said, "Wouldn't it be better if we prayed for God to save your husband and this other man's wife, rather than praying a 'let's kill 'em' prayer?" As hard as this is to believe, that thought had not actually occurred to them! Somehow they had become so ingrown in this prayer group that mass deception had set in, and they all became convinced of something that severely violated Scripture.[4]

Remember, if you don't think you can be deceived, you probably already are. Stay close to the Lord, His Word, and to godly, Bible-believing friends where there is healthy and appropriate accountability.

Soul Blockages

A soul blockage can be put in a similar category as inner vows, which we covered in the previous chapter. Soul blockages are what result from an inner vow. For instance, I was a preacher's kid, and like so many other PKs, when I was 18, I told myself I would never enter full-time ministry. I loved God, but I hated the church and had been very wounded by people who thought they had a wonderful plan for the preachers' kid (me)—yet, I could never do enough, serve enough, or be enough to meet their expectations.

Essentially, I had become shipwrecked. When I was 9 years old, God told me to preach the Gospel. Later on He came to me and gave me Psalm 2:8, telling me that I would one day preach in foreign nations. At that time, I had no idea what it meant to follow God or preach His word. In that sense, by the time I was 18, I had a soul block in this area.

God had to heal me concerning the church, which He so beautifully did not too many years later. What's fascinating is that God's timing is never off. Even though at 9 years old, I hadn't a clue what His prophetic word meant to me, the seed had been planted. You see, there's a process and timing; sometimes you might hear His voice and immediately be in a place to act upon it. At other times, what God is saying to you may be far beyond your own understanding. You may need to "mature into" the word of the Lord.

As I matured into my early 20s, I kept envisioning that little 9-year-old girl in the floral print dress, the voice of the Lord whispering to her like the soft wind through the oaks on a warm summer's eve. He was wooing me, you see—it was a process, and He knew that I had to go through some things in my life before I could fully accept His call.

In fact, it wasn't until I was 30 years old that I first preached the gospel. In my case, it took 21 years for that prophetic word to be activated. God called me when I was 9, and though I rejected Him when

I was 18, the calling was still there. I still felt its resonance deep inside; there was still something that made sense with the call of God.

The lesson I learned is that it is much better to respond to something rather than to react to something, as I had when I was 18. It's important that you check yourself, particularly if you are prone to "jumping the gun" and overreacting. If you have a soul blockage, or something is a hot button issue, you need to step back and say, "Why am I over-reacting rather than processing this in God?" There needs to be a balance between the inward witness of the Spirit and our own emotional or mental responses. It's possible that your wound is blocking you from receiving what God wants to do.

Also, I didn't want to preach the gospel because I was a woman. That was another soul blockage for me because I was raised in a culture that frowned upon women who preached. I wanted to be a Sunday school teacher or worship leader; I had a good deal of experience as a worship leader and a pianist, with a bachelor's degree and master's work in music education.

The last thing I wanted to do was travel and preach to the nations. I wrestled with God over that, and the Lord and I had a big fight. It was the word of the Lord, wasn't it? Yes. But what was the problem? My will didn't want to do what God was telling me to do. Has that ever happened to you? God says something to you, and you go, "Find somebody else. Get yourself another girl, God."

I went though a time of great struggle and actual misery. You know, when God tells you to do something, you might as well do it. You can go out the easy way or you can go out the hard way, but sooner or later, you're going to do it because He's God and you're not. That's it. Anyway, I was in my struggles because the word of the Lord was that God wanted me to preach. But I didn't know any woman preachers, which made the word that much more difficult. I had no one to talk to about being a woman preacher, so I was having a big conflict.

Then my husband became very obnoxious. (I mean that in a loving way, but at the time, I was not very happy with Mike!) He kept showing me the scripture in Galatians where it says, "there's neither male nor female" (Galatians 3:28). Mike kept saying, "I think God wants you to preach." And I kept saying, "No, Mike. God wants you to preach. You are the man; I am the woman. Let's figure this out."

For a time, I put my children to bed and walked the floor, crying. And I kept hearing these words. That's one way God will speak to you — over and over, as He tells you the same thing. It's like something gets stuck and you hear it over and over again, and what I heard was, "Cindy, I'm asking you to preach the gospel to the nations. I want you to go around the world and preach the gospel."

Well, I lived in the little town of Weatherford, Texas, and I wasn't interested in going around the world to preach the gospel. But there it was, the same verse over and over: "Ask of Me the nations for your inheritance, the ends of the earth for your possession" (Psalm 2:8). I just couldn't escape it.

Finally, one night at about two in the morning, I knelt down and said, "Lord, why do You want me as a woman? Why?" And He said, "So My prophecy will be fulfilled." I really did not have a good attitude and said, "Well, which prophecy is that? You have a lot of prophecies!" And He said, "And in the end times, I'll pour out My spirit on My sons and daughters. And if I'm going to pour out My spirit on my daughters, I'm going to need a few women! I choose you." (The Scripture that God spoke to me is from Joel 2:28, which is a powerful verse.)

Oh, God is so logical! Then He uses the Bible on you. Can you imagine that? I knelt down by our old blue velvet couch and lifted my hands to the Lord, saying, "Lord, alright. I surrender my life to go preach the gospel around the world. Here I am, Lord. Send me."

God just wants your availability. How could God take a little woman, a mother of two small children in a small town of 12,000, and send her around the world preaching the gospel? How could He do it? It's just by simply saying, "Here I am, Lord." See, God wanted that word He'd given to me at the tender age of nine to be fulfilled.

Sometimes the prophetic word will come, and it will be beyond your paradigm. Some people think that God won't tell you something you don't already know. Not true! The prophetic word is forth-telling; God will sometimes say things that are part of His destiny for you, but you just can't hear or understand. Why can't you see it? It's because there's something in your mind, will, or emotions that blocks it—a soul blockage.

God has a special plan just for you, and it might start as a very small seed deep, deep, deep inside you; nonetheless, it is a calling and it will grow. But we must be willing to let Him work. Perhaps it will happen for you as it did for me. God may give you a prophecy that lies dormant for many years, just waiting for the moment when you are finally ready and willing to see it, believe it, and move in it.

Dear one, the Holy Spirit is very interested in letting you know His will. As we give over our own dreams and desires, and surrender any soul blockages to Him, the Holy Spirit will be able to do His work.

Notes

3. Cindy Jacobs, *Possessing the Gates of the Enemy* (Grand Rapids: Chosen Books, 2009), 129-130.

4. Cindy Jacobs, *Possessing the Gates of the Enemy*, (Grand Rapids, Chosen Books, 2009), 131-132.

Chapter Six
How to Verify and Act Upon a Prophecy

It is a wonderful thing to grow in your ability to accurately hear God's voice and act upon what He is telling you. Hopefully some of the ideas in this short book will help you in that goal. But what if someone other than God speaks to you prophetically? How do you know whether or not a prophecy someone gives you is from God? That is a really important thing to know because if God is speaking to you, you will want to act, won't you? You will want to cooperate with what God is saying through that person.

It would be wonderful if everyone heard clearly and accurately from the Lord. But as we have seen in the previous couple of chapters, as broken human beings, there will be times when we don't hear with 100% accuracy. What this means is that we need safeguards—tools to hold us accountable and allow us to determine, with certainty, whether or not a word is from God. For example, sometimes only part of a prophetic message will be from the Lord, but not the whole thing. And this is true even if the one giving the prophecy ends with, "So says the Lord."

How then can we test a prophetic word? To be clear, we know that it's biblical to test the word. 1 Thessalonians 5:21 says, "Test all things. Hold fast what is good." Some people don't know how to test the word, and they get hurt. Then they wonder what happened or, even worse, tune out what God might truly want to say to them.

Let's look at some ways we can confirm a prophetic word that someone might give to us.

Is the Prophecy Scriptural?

The Scriptures are point A for our entire walk with God, aren't they? In Chapter 2, we discussed ways to know whether or not what you are hearing is from God or another source. When it comes to hearing from God through another person, similar principles apply.

First of all, is what has been shared as a prophetic word truly scriptural? God will never go against His word. Never. He will never tell you to do something that is against His character and nature. That's why it's important to be good students of scripture and to know what God's Word says.

I remember a prophet who fell into error and actually had women take off their clothes as he prophesied to them. Now, how he convinced those women to do that, I don't even have a clue! However, they probably just thought, "This is a prophet, and as a man of God, I can trust him." Of course, this is completely unscriptural.

Before I knew about these episodes, Mike and I had read a prophetic word from this same prophet. At one point the prophecy said, "I see the body of Christ like a naked woman." Mike and I exclaimed, "Uh, wait, stop! God is not going to show a male prophet a woman without her clothes on." There are some things that are just common sense. We know that God is never going to show you something that would cause you to fall into sin.

First and foremost: is the prophetic word scriptural?

Is There Fruit?

The second key is to examine what kind of fruit is being produced in the life of the person giving the prophetic word. There will be times, of course, when you might be at an event or conference and you won't know the person giving you the prophetic word. Therefore, because it would be impossible to know the fruit in their life, you must simply test the fruit of the word they give to you. Consult Galatians 5:22-23 as you pray through the word being given to you: "But the fruit of the Spirit is love, joy, peace, longsuffering, kindness, goodness, faithfulness, gentleness, self-control. Against such there is no law." Does the prophet exhibit these fruits?

Could you trust God to speak through a person who couldn't be trusted in the natural? No. Do they give their word and not keep their word? What is their character like? If God's going to trust them to carry His word, then they must be trustworthy in every area of their life. We need to let our yes be yes and our no be no, and work on being people of integrity and biblical ethics. This is the same for a person who wishes to give you a prophetic word.

Am I saying that unless the person lives a "perfect life" then their prophetic word to you is not to be believed or trusted? No. We are all fallen creatures. The main point I am making is to test the word and its source, and surrender the rest to the Holy Spirit.

Is Anything Tainting the Word?

Let's face it—we are impure vessels whom God has chosen to be His hands and feet on earth. We are multi-dimensional, imperfect, emotional beings who have good and bad days. We need to consider these realities when we measure a word that has been given to us by another person.

For example, oftentimes the person giving us a prophetic word may be a longtime friend or acquaintance. It's possible that if someone knows the past of a person in the natural, they may not be able to rise above what they know about that individual. Perhaps they only know about a major failure or moral lapse that occurred years ago, but not that the person repented and has since gotten their life back on track with God.

The danger is that the person prophesying may do so out of their human knowledge rather than out of God's knowledge. Can you see that? If that is the case, the given prophetic word can be destructive or angry and may get in the way of what God actually wants to say. The best way to test such a word—one that is given to you but feels a bit "off"—is to pray for God's wisdom and share it with trusted friends who know your entire history. In the end, God's truth will prevail.

Never forget that you have the Holy Spirit within you. It is always good to remember that it is kindness that leads us to repentance (Romans 2:4).

Is the Person Critical or Judgmental?

A critical spirit will come through in a person's prophetic style because they will focus on the negative rather than the positive. Such a negative approach is harmful and can wound the human spirit. Did you know it's possible for someone to give what they say is a word of the Lord, yet it can nonetheless erode or attack your personhood?

Psalm 23 is perhaps David's most beloved Psalm. In verse 3, David says, "He restores my soul." Our God is a restorative God. If you receive a prophetic word that damages your soul, you need to weigh it and ask for God to sift out the truth. Again, perhaps part of the message is truly from God, but not all. A prophetic word should exhort you, it should comfort you, and it should lift you up. It shouldn't damage you. And though sometimes the prophetic word might convict or challenge you, it will always be restorative.

Is There An Inner Witness of the Spirit?

Because we receive the Holy Spirit upon our conversion to Christ, we can trust His voice within us. When you receive a prophetic word from a source other than God or the Bible, you need to surrender it and ask the Holy Spirit to give you resonance. We talked about this in Chapter Two, but it is very relevant here as well.

For me, John 14 is one of the most poignant chapters in the Bible. It is just after the Last Supper, and Jesus is comforting His apostles, preparing them for the inevitable time when He will go to be with the Father. Christ knows He will soon depart and encourages them, saying,

> And I will pray the Father, and He will give you another Helper, that He may abide with you forever—the Spirit of truth, whom the world cannot receive, because it neither sees Him nor knows Him; but you know Him, for He dwells with you and will be in you.
>
> JOHN 14:16-17

I don't know about you, but it is difficult for me to read that passage without getting a little emotional. It is such a loving, intimate, caring expression of assurance from Jesus to those whom He loves. In essence, He is saying that though He needs to depart, the Holy Spirit will be with them. And that, my friends, is our assurance: the Holy Spirit will, indeed, know you, dwell with you, and be in you. You can trust Him to divide the word and help you discern the veracity of a prophetic word given to you by another.

Is There An Outer Witness?

As we have already discussed, God will confirm His word by the mouths of two or three witnesses (see 2 Corinthians 13:1). There is, indeed, assurance in numbers. Lest we forget, Christ confirms this when He says, "For where two or three are gathered together in My name, I am there in the midst of them" (see Matthew 18:20).

Because God is a loving, jealous God, He will continue to pursue us with His word. If you don't get the prophecy the first time, He'll send it a second time. He may use a close friend, the scriptures, His voice, or circumstances in your life—but rest assured, He will send the word again. God has a loud voice, and He will keep telling you over and over. Of course, sometimes there is timing in what He's trying to tell you.

Because Mike and I are married and in ministry together, there are times where we don't see things exactly the same way. (Shocking, I'm sure.) At times as leaders, we just don't have an agreement between us, so we consult our Board of Directors. We have people we trust who pray for us, and we often consult with them to make sure we are on track.

This is very practical, but it has kept us in good standing. As the Lord told me, "If you are under authority, you will be a person of great authority." Be willing to seek advice, and find some people you can walk with who will help confirm the word to you.

Will This Damage My Family?

When God is prophesying to you, He will not lead you to do something that will damage your family. If God is calling you to do something and you have a spouse and children, God will also begin to minister and prepare them for what He's saying to you. Remember I said God has collective hearing? It used to be that one spouse would drag the other along, and they wouldn't hear God together. Or a missionary would take their family into the mission field, and they'd all be kicking and screaming.

But I believe that God gives grace, and as we pray, He is able to speak from the youngest to the oldest. I wish we'd better understood this principle when our children were little because I believe we need to dream together as a family for the vision of God. Of course, there may be things that God leads you and your spouse to do that will be beyond the understanding or maturity level of your children.

But still, rather than simply saying you've made the decision and the kids are just going to need to get on board, you can approach it as Christ would—in an uplifting, loving way. I wish we had called our children together and said, "This is something God is really speaking to us. Can we pray through this together?"

I think we need to broaden our thinking in the way God wants to use family units. One of the reasons I rebelled against the call of God in my life had to do with not feeling like my opinion mattered in some major decisions. As a child, I remember my Dad coming in and saying, "Well, we're going to another church. I've accepted the call in another place, so get in the car. We're packing up, and we're going to move."

I didn't have time to process such a startling turn of events. It was very hard to just yank up stakes, leave friends behind, and move to another town. Do I believe my Dad heard from God and that the Lord had called my Dad to different pastoral positions? Yes. However, it was hard to move all the time, especially when I didn't feel like I was included in the decision. Don't get me wrong; I had wonderful, supportive parents. I only can do what I do today because they gave me such confidence and support. However, my family didn't understand that God works in community.

Give time for your family to process major moves and decisions with you. If possible, allow for time to just pray through things, and let God work through the relationships around you.

If God gives you a prophetic word, you need to understand that not only will God speak to you, but to others around you—people that care for you. Mike and I are under the authority of our wonderful pastor, Jim Hennesy, at Trinity Church, outside Dallas. We frequently consult with him, both on minor and major decisions. And even when we are on the road, we try to call him often. We have learned that God has given us massive authority because we have learned to humble ourselves and ask for help, advice, and prayer.

Assess the Timing of a Word

Not only do you need to test the word that is given to you, but also you need to assess the timing of the word. For everything that God does, there is a time and a season (see Ecclesiastes 3). And quite honestly, this is where many people miss the fullness of the word being given. I can look back at times over the years where I just missed the timing of a word—by either moving too early or too late. How then do we discern the proper timing of the word?

As with the accuracy of a word, we discern the timing of a word by consulting the scriptures, praying, seeking wise counsel, and making sure that the word is not tainted. At times, as we've discussed, other people's imperfections or sinfulness may mess up the timing a bit. However, that is when God redeems the time (see Ephesians 5:16). It is in such broken situations where we must meditate on Romans 8:28: "And we know that all things work together for good to those who love God, to those who are the called according to His purpose."

On numerous occasions, Mike has shared about when he was laid off from his position at American Airlines. The company went through a huge series of layoffs and then brought in B-pay scale employees. They paid these employees a lot less, while the A-pay scale employees were all furloughed. At the time of the layoff, we were in the planning stages of launching Generals International, but we thought the launch was still two years away. Our children would have been a bit older, and we would have been able to save a little money. But suddenly—and more abruptly than we had wanted—we were thrown out of the boat.

Whether or not an unfortunate circumstance is caused by the

enemy, your own choices, or the sinful nature of people in your life, God always has a plan B. Determine that you need to just step out in faith, as Mike and I had to do. And then ask God to give you the measure of faith needed for where you are. And sure enough, He will be faithful.

God will be faithful.

Chapter Seven

God Wants to Speak to You!

My goal in these pages has been to help you know that God still speaks today. He loves you so much that He is yearning to open up a two-way conversation with you. I pray and trust that this small book has given you some new tools to do just that.

I wanted to close by recapping some of the key steps we can take to hear God more clearly in a world that assaults our senses every day. The following ten points are a summary of what we have discussed and can help you stay on track as you refer back to the key sections of the book:

1. God loves you and yearns to speak to you. Even if you've never heard God's voice before, or never even knew He still speaks today, He is waiting for you to hear His voice. Our theme verse for this truth is John 18:37.

2. God desires intimacy with you. Beyond just entering into a two-way conversation, God's desire is to fill you with His love and peace. Are you ready to let Him in? See 1 Corinthians 14:1.

3. Many people do believe that God still speaks today but assume that only a person seated in the office of prophet can hear from God. That is not true or biblical! While only a certain number of people are prophets, all Christians are capable of prophesying. See 1 Corinthians 14 and in particular, verses 1-5 and 39.

4. As you begin to tune your ear to hear God more clearly, ensure that all you do is based on God's Word. This will help you to discern the origin of the word and to make sure that it truly is biblical and from God. See 1 John 4:1-6.

5. Surround yourself with godly, Bible-believing Christians who can mentor you and help you in your quest to hear God more clearly and accurately.

6. Ask the Holy Spirit to give you an inner witness as to the accuracy of what you think you are hearing from God. See John 10:27-29.

7. Understand the three major functions of prophecy, as outlined in 1 Corinthians 14:3: edification (edify, build up, and renovate), exhortation (help, educate, instruct), and comfort (soothe, bring peace, empathize).

8. In order to fully hear the voice of God and discern His destiny for you, it's critical to heal any wounds from your past, including being shipwrecked emotionally, breaking inner vows, overcoming disappointments, forgiving yourself, and accepting God's grace and mercy. See 1 Timothy 1:18-20, 2 Corinthians 5:17, 1 Peter 2:24, Romans 11:29, Mark 4:9, 1 John 3:22, Matthew 19:26, Isaiah 53:5, Luke 22:7, Matthew 11:29, Psalm 103:2, Romans 8:28, and Zechariah 4:10.

9. As we heal from past wounds and allow God's voice to more deeply and clearly penetrate our mind and spirit, we need to remove any remaining obstacles in our way. Such roadblocks can include unmet expectations, disobedience and sin, unbelief, bitterness, spiritual warfare, self-deception, and soul blockages. Key verses in clearing such hurdles include John 3:4, Mark 29:23-24, Luke 17:6, Hebrews 11.

10. It is crucial that we verify the accuracy of a prophetic word given to us by another person and then act upon that word. We must consider the following: Is the word scriptural? Does the person giving the word display the fruits of the Spirit (Galatians 5:22-23)? Is anything tainting the word—is the goodness of God within the word (Romans 2:4)? Is the word being brought in a critical or harsh spirit, or is it restorative (Psalm 23:3)? Do you have an inner witness from the Holy Spirit (John 14:16-17)? Does the word resonate with two or more

witnesses (2 Corinthians 13:1, Matthew 18:20)? Does the word follow in God's timing as you discern it (Ecclesiastes 3)?

Finally, dear ones, I want to thank you for your courage. Does that sound like a strange thing to say? Maybe. But in this world, where there are so many voices vying for our attention, it takes a purposeful, determined, on-going effort to focus on God's voice. It takes courage! It is difficult to hear God's voice above the noise, isn't it? But as you press into the Holy Spirit and pursue the Lord, He will also pursue you. And like with any close friend, after a time, you will begin to recognize the tone and timbre of His voice.

When you are having "one of those days" and struggling to just make it through to lunch (let alone hear God's voice above the din!), be assured that His plans for you are both wonderful and real.

In closing, I leave you with a scripture that I trust will reassure you of the Father's love and the wonder of His destiny for you:

> Let not your heart be troubled; you believe in God, believe also in Me. In My Father's house are many mansions; if it were not so, I would have told you. I go to prepare a place for you. And if I go and prepare a place for you, I will come again and receive you to Myself; that where I am, there you may be also. And where I go you know, and the way you know.
>
> JOHN 14:1-4

About the Author

Cindy Jacobs is an author, speaker, and teacher with a heart for discipling nations in the areas of prayer and prophetic gifts. She and Mike—her husband of 41 years—co-founded Generals International in 1985. At nine years old, the Lord called Cindy when He urged her to read Psalm 2:8: "Ask of me the nations for your inheritance, and the ends of the world for your possession." That small seed God planted many years ago has sprouted and grown into an international ministry, taking Cindy to more than 100 nations of the world, where she has spoken before hundreds of thousands, including many heads of nations.

Cindy helps people walk in the ministry of prophetic intercession, equipping them to pray effectively for their families, cities, and nations. She describes her call to the nations as "an inverted homesickness": while she has strong bonds with her two children and six grandchildren back home in Dallas, she has a constant yearning to minister to unreached people globally. Through her journeys, Cindy's heart has remained fixed on the realization that Jesus left the ninety-and-nine to go to the one.

Cindy has written for *Charisma*, *Ministry Today*, and *Spirit-Led Woman*, and is the author of seven books, including such bestsellers as *Possessing the Gates of the Enemy*, *The Voice of God*, and *Women of Destiny*. She is a frequent guest on Trinity Broadcasting Network and *The 700 Club*, and together with Mike, co-hosts *God Knows*, a weekly television show that has aired to a potential audience of 800 million people in more than 200 nations in five different languages. Cindy earned her B.A. in Music from Pepperdine University and also completed graduate work in Music from Pepperdine. She holds honorary doctorates from Asian Theological Association for her work with unreached people groups, and from Christian International in Santa Rosa Beach, FL.

About Generals International

Generals International (GI) is a prayer-based organization founded by Mike and Cindy Jacobs in 1985 that exists for the purpose of changing lives and transforming nations. We are passionate about the message that God cares about every individual, He cares about every nation, and He still speaks to us today. Out of that passion, we develop resources to equip believers in areas such as:

- Prayer & Intercession

- Prophecy & Spiritual Warfare

- The Holy Spirit & the Supernatural

- Reconciliation & Reformation

We invite you to join our community of Generals, a place where we offer a solid foundation on which to build your faith and spiritual gifts. As we walk together through daily life, we want you to realize your identity and do extraordinary things that will ultimately fulfill the will of God in the nations.

And why do we want to make Generals? Because we embrace the principle of multiplication. We impart the message of changing lives to you, and through your impact on countless others, the nations are transformed.

To find more, visit www.generals.org.

More Books by Cindy Jacobs

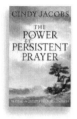

The Power of Persistent Prayer
Praying with Greater Purpose and Passion

Discover what Cindy Jacobs has learned through her years of powerful, persistent prayer and now shares, including: the basics of prayer, praying the word, fasting, praise, intercession, and more.

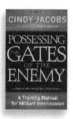

Possessing The Gates of The Enemy
A Training Manual for Militant Intercession

This book is a wealth of information on prayer and intercession. It covers everything from the call to intercession, conducting "spiritual mapping" and praying to break strongholds over your city. This book is a definite for interceessors, pastors, and other spiritual leaders to understand the depths involved in spiritual warfare.

The Voice of God
How God Speaks Personally and Corporately to His Children Today

This Book cuts through the confusion about prophecy and provides and uplifting, biblical picturefor hearing and acting upon our Master's voice. This book will teach you to hear and discern God's whispers, so He can greatly use you to minister to a hurting world.

Women of Destiny
Releasing Women to Fulfill God's Call in their Lives and in the Church

Using scripture, true-life stories of God's greatest heroines, and her personal journey in answering God's call, Cindy encourages all Christian women to accept His calling and take a more active part in ministering to others. She sends a clear, uplifting message that will help you find the boldness, vision, and confidence to live the life God intended for you.

44633823R00044

Made in the USA
Charleston, SC
02 August 2015